# THE modern cottage COLLECTION

## COLORING BOOK

instagram: @jenracinecoloring

facebook.com/jenracinecoloring

www.jenracine.com

## Hello Coloring Friends!

Thank you for purchasing this book. I sincerely hope that you find enjoyment and contentment in these pages! In addition to new illustrations, this collection has a selection of drawings found in a few of my other books, Scandi Nature, Time to Hygge and Garden Gnomes. I have modified and changed them to reflect a modern cottage aesthetic but they are similar to previous versions. Happy coloring!

## Tips for Coloring

This paper is best suited for colored pencil or gel pens. Markers have a tendency to bleed through. For all media, it's best to put one or several pieces of paper behind the page to prevent bleed-through and creasing on the next page.

**Find all JEN RACINE coloring books in online bookstores.**

Find coloring pages on **Etsy**:
JenRacineColoring

ISBN: 978-1-951728-56-4

JAM

Made in the USA
Middletown, DE
29 March 2023

27929825R00046